JAMESTOWN TRIVIA!

Flabbergasting Facts for Kids ...and Adults!

Who would've guessed?

ARE YOU KIDDING?

Did You know?

SURELY YOU jest!

by Carole Marsh

Jamestown
First Permanent English Settlement in the New World

Copyright ©2006 Carole Marsh/ Gallopade International
All rights reserved.
First Edition

Published by Gallopade International/Carole Marsh Books.
Printed in the United States of America.

Managing Editor: Sherry Moss
Editorial Assistant: Rachel Moss
Cover Design: Michele Winkelman
Content Design: Randolyn Friedlander

Gallopade is proud to be a member and supporter of these
educational organizations and associations:
American Booksellers Association
International Reading Association
National Association for Gifted Children
The National School Supply and Equipment Association
The National Council for the Social Studies
Museum Store Association
Association of Partners for Public Lands

Table of Contents

The Ships...

In 1607, three ships set sail across the Atlantic for England to establish Jamestown, the first permanent English settlement in the New World! They were the Susan Constant, the Godspeed, and the Discovery. The ships were small and it was a tight squeeze to fit all 144 men and boys on board!

The three ships that sailed across the Atlantic were not meant to carry passengers but to carry cargo.

Along with the colonists and crew, the three ships held provisions, tools and parts for a smaller boat that would be assembled in Virginia and used for inland exploration!

FLOUR

AR

Almost immediately after
the ships left for sea, they
were stuck in the English
Channel for a month!
Storms and unfavorable
winds kept them from
heading out!

The sailors used compasses to measure direction. Each compass was put into a wooden box held together by wooden pegs. Metal nails could not be used because the magnetism would alter the results!

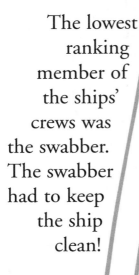

The lowest ranking member of the ships' crews was the swabber. The swabber had to keep the ship clean!

Although it was not an official title, there was still one person aboard each ship whose rank was lower than the swabber and that was the liar. Each week the first person caught in a lie would be sentenced to clean the beakhead – the part of the ship where the other crew members used the bathroom!

On board each ship there
was a sealed box containing
the Virginia Company's
instructions to the colonists
and names of the settlement's
leaders. The instructions
were to be opened only after
the ships had arrived in
Virginia–and not before.

So did they peek or didn't they?!

The commander of
the Susan Constant was
Christopher Newport,
a privateer who raided
Spanish ships. Newport
was one of England's
most experienced and
distinguished mariners!

The Susan
Constant
held cannons
that were to
be used in case of
pirate attacks!

You might say that Newport led the Jamestown voyage "single-handedly," having lost his right arm during an attack off the coast of Cuba!

Of the three ships' captains, only Christopher Newport did not die in Virginia!

In 1605, knowing
that King James
was fascinated by
exotic animals,
Christopher Newport
brought back to him
two baby crocodiles
and a wild boar from
Caribbean waters!

In January of 1608,
Christopher Newport
returned to Jamestown
in a ship called the
John and Francis.
Aboard this ship
were fresh supplies
and almost
60 new colonists!

The **Godspeed** was under
the command of Bartholomew
Gosnold, an Englishman who
explored Cape Cod and
Martha's Vineyard.
Martha's Vineyard was
named after Gosnold's
firstborn daughter who
had died at a young age!

Edward-Maria Wingfield was a wealthy investor who traveled on one of the ships. He was the Jamestown colony's first president, but after less than a year went back to England. He was voted out of office by unhappy colonists.

Some folks believed he kept food for himself while others were starving!

The Journey...

England was known for its irksome privateers—government-licensed pirates—who looted Spanish cargo ships!

In 1606, England's explorations did not compare to those of Portugal and Spain who had already colonized many parts of the western world. England was not considered a colonial power. Most people of the day would never have believed that England would eventually occupy and control most of North America!

The Virginia Company, who funded the Jamestown colony, hoped for a peaceful relationship between the colonists and the natives. The colonists were told to settle on land that was not already inhabited by the Indians.

The crossing of the Atlantic was
in trouble from the start.
Before setting sail, they saw
Halley's Comet cross the night sky!
It was considered to be bad luck!

The six weeks braving bad
weather off the Bristish coast
cost the colonists provisions
that they would later need
to survive!

The sailors landed in Dominica to get more food and water. When they arrived they met up with natives who wore jewelry through their ears, lips and noses – but no other clothing. The men and the women spoke different languages and the sailors were extremely cautious because they had heard that the Caribs (the Dominican people) sometimes ate human flesh!

On the island of Nevis, the English's biggest
enemy was a tree called the manchineel.
The manchineel has leafy branches and fruit
that looks like apples. But beware! The touch
of the manchineel's sap is like acid and burns
the victim's skin. The fruit is poisonous too!

–but beware–

On the island of Mona, the sailors stopped to replenish their water supply. While there, some men went off on a hunting expedition and killed boars and iguanas.

The iguanas were five to six feet long!

Iguanas go to Jamestown, too, please!

The ships' last stop before they reached Virginia was the island of Monito. When the men arrived, they found that the island was already inhabited—by a huge flock of wildfowl! The sailors weren't able to set foot on the ground without stepping on birds or eggs! The men caught the birds with their hands and filled two barrels with them!

Of all the gull!

On Arrival...

The Jamestown colony was established to make money from the gold, silver, and other riches that were thought to be in that region of North America. The colonists were also expected to discover a passage to the Orient—

of course there wasn't any!

The majority of the colonists who came on the ships died within months due to disease, hunger and hostile natives!

Jamestown survived thanks to two people,
a commoner and a royal.

The commoner was Captain John Smith and
the royal was Pocahontas, daughter of the most
powerful chief in Virginia, Wahunsonacock,
better known as Chief Powhatan!

POCAHONTAS

Pocahontas was only eleven years old when
she befriended John Smith and gave him and
the other newcomers crucial assistance.

John Smith credited her with saving the colony!

John Smith had dreamed
of going overseas ever since
he was a young boy but his
father stopped him. When he
was 16 or 17, his father died
and John Smith was free to
head to sea. He did and changed
the course of history!

John Smith's motto was
"To overcome is to Live!"

John Smith taught himself how to be a good soldier by reading books and studying. He even became an explosives expert with the help of a book!

John Smith was once captured on a Romanian battlefield and sold into slavery. He was told that escape was impossible, and that was all he needed to hear to decide he was going to escape! One day when his master came by, Smith killed him and rode off on the dead master's horse!

When the sailors arrived
it was late April and Virginia's
forests were full of white dogwoods.
It must have been a much prettier
sight than looking at the endless ocean
for months and months!

When the sailors finally came to the Chesapeake Bay they stopped and raised a cross, thankful that they had arrived!

The first day
after the
English
arrived in Virginia,
they explored
the land. While they were on
their way back to the ships, they
were followed by natives.

The natives attacked with arrows
and shot a sailor named Gabriel Archer
in both hands and another sailor,
Mathew Morton, in several places on
his body.

Both men survived!

One of the instructions in the
sealed boxes was that the colonists
"have great care not to offend the
naturals" — natives, that is.
The colonists were told to
begin trading with the Virginia Indians
immediately for food, just in case
their corn didn't do well.
And guess what?!

The first natives the colonists had any positive interaction with were the Kecoughtans. They wore animal skin coverings decorated with bones and animal teeth and their bodies were painted black and red. They wore bird legs in their ears and their hair was shaved on the right side, but left to grow three to four feet long on the left side!

Gabriel Archer spotted a possible
place to found the colony.
The colonists called it Archer's Hope.
It was thought to be a good place to
settle because it had a view of the
river that would let the colonists see
ships miles downstream and, it
was full of rabbits, turkeys and
turkey eggs!

Edward-Maria Wingfield did not
think Archer's Hope was the best
place to settle. He preferred a
peninsula with very deep water
where the colonists' ships could
easily pull up. Christopher
Newport also thought the peninsula
was the better place of the two.
So the men landed there and
later named it James Town!

Out of six men, Edward-Maria Wingfield was chosen as the first president for a one-year term at Jamestown. Wingfield decided not to build a fort and not to use weapons. In doing so, Wingfield left the colony defenseless! Instead, they built a fort almost immediately!

The Virginia Indians...

The English saw the natives as "savages" and used that as their everyday term for them!

The English believed that the natives were actually born as white people and then their skin changed colors as an effect from the dyes they used to decorate themselves and ward off mosquitoes!

Chief Powhatan had inherited
six tribes from his father and
conquered at least 22 more.
Each tribe had to give
him 80 percent of
everything they grew,
caught or made!

In 1607, Chief
Powhatan's empire
covered all of modern-day
eastern Virginia spreading
down to what is now the
Virginia-North Carolina
line!

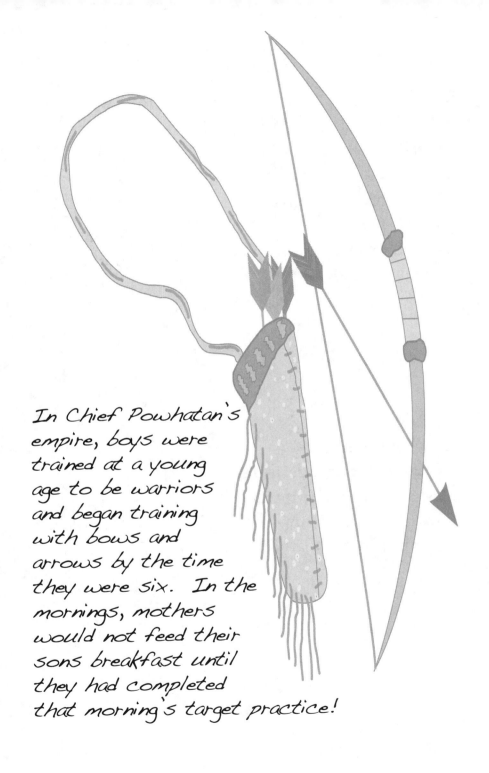

In Chief Powhatan's empire, boys were trained at a young age to be warriors and began training with bows and arrows by the time they were six. In the mornings, mothers would not feed their sons breakfast until they had completed that morning's target practice!

Shortly before the English arrived, one of Powhatan's priests prophesied that a nation would arise from the Chesapeake Bay and overcome his empire. The English came from the Chesapeake Bay, and soon, Chief Powhatan and his advisers would have to decide if they were the subjects of that prophecy!

During an attack from the natives,
Edward-Maria Wingfield felt an arrow
pass harmlessly through his beard!
C...c...c...close call!

Surrounding James Fort was tall
grass where the enemy natives
would hide for surprise attacks.
The natives that were the friends
of the colonists made the suggestion
to cut the grass!
Duh!

The emperor Powhatan was old and gray-haired, but had the body of a younger man. He was tall and fit. On his chin were the remains of a thinning beard!

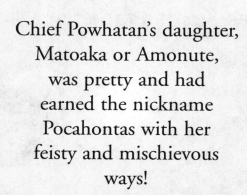

Chief Powhatan had at least 100 wives!

Chief Powhatan's daughter, Matoaka or Amonute, was pretty and had earned the nickname Pocahontas with her feisty and mischievous ways!

When Chief Powhatan got word that
Christopher Newport had come back
to Jamestown, he sent many gifts.
Half of the gifts were for Smith and
half for Smith's "father."
(Chief Powhatan believed that
because Newport had been described
to him as a man of great power, he
was Smith's father!)

Chief Powhatan invited John Smith
and Christopher Newport to his
village because he wanted to meet
Newport. Newport gave Chief
Powhatan a suit of red cloth, a hat
and a white greyhound dog.
Powhatan liked the dog best of all!

To go deer hunting, groups of native men would gather and find a herd around which they would build fires. The deer were too scared of the fires to run out of the circle, which made them easy targets!

The natives built their own canoes. It was not an easy task! First, the natives had to hollow out a large log by partially burning it. Then they formed the shape by scraping the log inside and out with oyster shells and stone tools!

Sometimes Powhatan hunters covered themselves in deerskins with stuffed heads to disguise themselves!

The Powhatan men were skilled hunters, fishermen and warriors!

The Powhatan women and children worked very hard! They did everything from planting and harvesting to making baskets and clay pots!

Women and children roamed their territory every day. They had to go out of the village to do most of their work such as collecting water, or gathering firewood, plants and clay for pottery!

While mothers worked, they carried their babies on cradleboards to keep their babies warm and secure for the first few months of their lives. Cradleboards often had a hoop over the head area to protect the baby from injury and an awning for shelter from sun and rain.

A dependable source of food for the Native Americans and the settlers was the Virginia white-tailed deer!

It is believed that more Indians died from diseases the English had brought with them to Jamestown than they did from gunfire!

In 1613, Pocahontas was captured and held prisoner by the English to try and get the Powhatans to stop attacking Jamestown. While being held prisoner, she met a colonist named John Rolfe. They were married in 1614 and the marriage brought peace between the Indians and the English for eight years!

During times of peace, the Indians showed the colonists how to cultivate beans, squash and corn. They also taught the settlers how to hunt deer and wild turkey and to catch fish in traps!!

Hey, farmer, I'm a turkey–but I'm not wild!

The Powhatan Indians treasured copper the way the English treasured gold. The Powhatan Indians often fought with the Monacan tribe, which was their main source of copper. Judging by the amount of copper scraps that have been found, a jeweler in Jamestown must have been busy making copper items to trade with the Indians. Copper may have helped to save Jamestown from the Indians in the first years!

When Powhatan children were born, they were given a formal name. When they got older, they received more personal names!

Children were loved not only by their parents, but by the whole community! This is sort of like today when we say "It takes a village to raise a child."

The Saga Continues...

Once Newport left Jamestown on
June 22 with the sailors
who had done a lot of work for the
colony, conditions got bad in
Jamestown. Food spoiled and
provisions ran low. Some men
didn't know what to do, and just
wanted to wait for Newport to
return with supplies and workers.

But that was going to be 6 months!

Daily food rations for each
colonist was a half pint of barley
boiled in water and a half pint of wheat.
Both were crawling with worms!
Yikes!

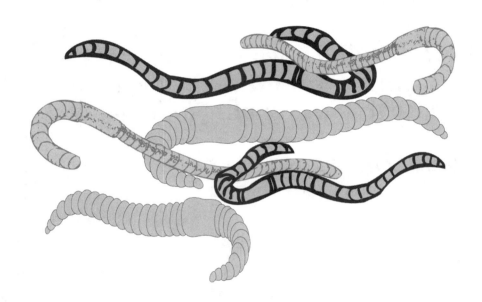

The men quickly began to die of
diseases and hunger. Those who
were not sick took turns standing
guard and burying the bodies of the dead!

When so many of the men were sick,
they expected the natives to come
and finish them off. Instead,
the natives began to bring the
colonists corn and other products
from a recent harvest to trade.
It was enough to get the surviving
men back on their feet!

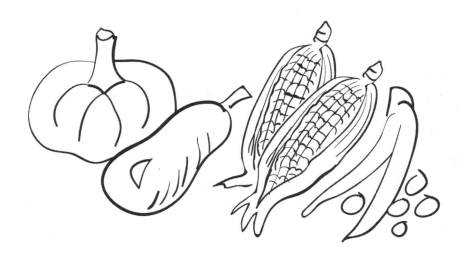

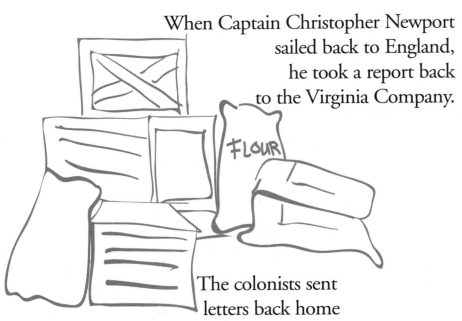

When Captain Christopher Newport
sailed back to England,
he took a report back
to the Virginia Company.

FLOUR

The colonists sent
letters back home
with Newport but each letter was
screened to make sure that it did not
say anything negative about the colony!

Winter brought geese, ducks and
other fowl to the rivers, providing
plentiful game for the colonists to hunt!

John Ratcliffe became the colony's president after Wingfield left office. Ratcliffe put John Smith in charge of building houses and relations with the natives. It was Smith's job to figure out how to maintain a friendship with the natives and trade with them!

Because of his military background, John Smith was good at learning languages. Smith became one of the colony's most effective speakers of Algonquian, the Indians' language!

John Smith was captured by the Powhatan, and he asked that messengers take a written message back to the James Fort telling the colonists to send certain things back with the natives. When the colonists sent back exactly what John Smith had said they would, the natives were amazed. They had no written language and decided that the English could make paper talk!

Ok, paper—what do you have to say for yourself?

As a prisoner, John Smith was led in front of Chief Powhatan to have his fate decided. The great chief was seated on mats and wore a raccoon skin robe with the tails still attached and chains of pearls hanging from his neck!

!!!
...

When John Smith made it back to Jamestown after his encounter with Chief Powhatan, he was blamed for the deaths of Thomas Emry and Jehu Robinson, two men who had been ambushed while under Smith's care. Lucky for John Smith, on the day he was to be executed, Christopher Newport arrived back at Jamestown and took control!

I wonder if they would have given him a blindfold?

We will never know!

Newport had taken what he thought to be gold back to England where it was proven to be only fool's gold. As part of Newport's mission back to Jamestown, he was to find real gold and bring it back to England!

Real or fool's?

John Smith sent a manuscript he had written back to England. The manuscript had more than 13,000 words recounting the events that had happened on the journey, from beginning to end. It was published and made available to the public under the title of *A True Relation of Such Occurrences and Accidents of Note as Hath Hapned in Virginia Since the First Planting of that Colony, which is now resident in the South part thereof, till the last returne from thence.*

What a title!

At the time of the founding of Jamestown, it was traditional for explorers to name the places they found after kings, queens and princes. As Smith and his men explored, they did not do that. They often named places for themselves, or other English sailors and settlers.

Winds, lightning and rains forced John Smith and his fellow explorers to spend two days on an island that they ended up calling Limbo!

John Smith's "explorations" were made up of trying to get in good with the Indians, making bargains and trades, dealing with disease, and discouraging enemy attacks.

John Smith took an oath of office as the president of Jamestown on September 10, 1608!

I feel safe now!

He's "the man!"

When John Smith became president of Jamestown, his first rule to the surviving colonists was "He that will not worke shall not eat!"

In the fall of 1609, Smith suffered a serious wound from a gunpowder accident. Afraid he would not live, he sailed back to England. He never returned to Jamestown, but explored the New England area years later.

In the first dozen years of the Jamestown colony, colonists faced a one in eight chance of staying alive!

The first women of Jamestown were
Mistress Forrest and her maid,
Anne Burras. Mistress Forrest
was with her husband Thomas,
leaving Anne Burras as the only
single woman in the middle of
200 men! Anne was won over by
John Laydon and they were
married in no time!

The colonists planted tobacco and soon
it became the way to financial success
in the colony. This milder-tasting tobacco
became very popular in England!
The demand was so great that even the
streets of Jamestown had sprouting
tobacco plants.

On John Smith's expeditions along the rivers in Virginia he made remarkably accurate maps and charts of the Virginia coastline!

Many of the first group of men who arrived in Jamestown were people not used to physical labor. It soon became clear that, like it or not, everyone had to pitch in for the colony to survive!

There were many reasons why people risked everything to come to Virginia. Some had an urgent need to leave England, some believed the promise that America held a better life, and some wanted to help the colony thrive because they had invested money in the venture.

Eventually, almost all of the settlers of the Jamestown colony were recruited from the working class such as carpenters, masons and other skilled craftsmen.

Although the colonists wanted to leave England, they did not want to stop being English. They tried very hard to recreate an England in Jamestown and to have the same customs and way of life as they did back home!

The English craftsmen and carpenters made homes according to what they knew from England, where wood was scarce. Houses were made of "mud and stud," a mixture of twigs and sticks covered with mud and clay.

The Rest of the Story...

Jamestown was officially called "London's Plantation in the Southern Part of Virginia!"

The survival of Jamestown,
and even Virginia, is very much
thanks to the corn that provided
a staple for the new settlers.
Some kinds of corn matured early
while other kinds could be harvested
late to provide food when the woods
and streams provided little!

So always count your corn blessings!

Jamestown was the capital of
Virginia from 1607 to 1699.
The fourth and last statehouse at
Jamestown burned in 1698, giving
those who thought the capital should
be elsewhere a chance to move
the capital. The capital was eventually
moved to Williamsburg.

When Jamestown became the capital,
it caused more conflict between royal
authority and the independent
Virginians. The colonists, who had to
fend for and protect themselves, didn't
see any reason to be controlled by
anyone outside the colony.

Can you blame them?!

It wasn't until 1907 that Jamestown began to receive national and international attention.

A monument commemorating the 300th anniversary in that year still stands on the island today!

The women of Jamestown worked very hard. They planted, harvested and preserved food, made clothes and took care of what farm animals were available. Their work was never done!

The women who came over to Jamestown from England included servants and single women. Some single women became the wives of men who were willing to pay for their trip from England!

In the early years of Jamestown, for every one woman there were four men!

If a servant girl was bought by a small farmer, she would probably find herself cultivating tobacco. If a large family with many male servants bought a girl servant, she would probably be given the chores of cooking, washing and helping the housewife!

NEWCOMERS TO JAMESTOWN OFTEN HAD TO GO THROUGH "SEASONING"— CATCHING AND SURVIVING THE DISEASES OF THE NEW COLONY.

MORE ENGLISH PEOPLE DIED FROM DISEASE THAN FROM INDIAN ATTACKS!

The settlers did not harvest their first crop of corn until the fall of 1609! That was more than two years after they landed!

"The Starving Time" was the winter of 1609-1610, when bitter cold weather and lack of food left only 60 colonists alive!

Most of the time, even when crops of corn were needed, tobacco would be planted instead because it was the money-maker of the colony!

Within six years, the soil where the tobacco had been planted year after year after year was exhausted!

You would be too!

The first documented Africans
arrived in Virginia in 1619.
They were captured during war
with the Portuguese. These first
Africans were treated as indentured
servants, meaning they could work
to earn their freedom.

The first representative government began at Jamestown in 1619 with the convening of a general assembly. The Virginia Company was done away with in 1624 and Virginia became a royal colony.

Although John Smith never returned to Jamestown, he spent much of his time in England promoting the colonization of North America until his death in 1631. He also wrote and published many accounts of Jamestown.

JOHN SMITH

The Anglican Church was the church of the Virginia colony.

In 1607, settlers built a church inside the fort at Jamestown. It was a barn-like structure and the settlers worshiped in it until it was destroyed in a fire in January 1608!

The Jamestown Colony, which was thought to be lost to the currents of the James River, was rediscovered in 1994 by an archaeologist named William Kelso. Much of the colony and the fort have been unearthed.

More than one million artifacts have been found that have helped reveal the roots of what would become the United States of America! The archaeologists tease that the artifacts are getting in the way of the mud!

The fort at Jamestown was a wooden triangle with circular watchtowers at each corner. Inside the fort was a storehouse, many houses and a church. Archaeologists have found the three sides of the fort, a moat, a dungeon, and burial sites!

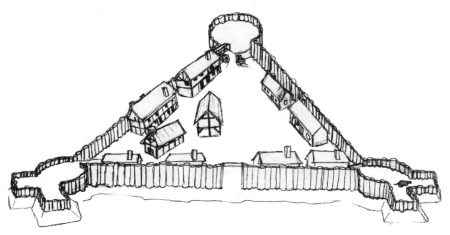

One of the reasons the colonists chose the Jamestown site was because it was easy to defend from enemies. But, it was a poor choice for a settlement because it was low, swampy and the perfect breeding ground for mosquitoes that carried diseases such as malaria!

But a guy's gotta eat!

When John Smith went back to England
in 1609 there were seven horses
at Jamestown. They were eaten by the
colonists during the Starving Time!

**The early settlers
often had turtle as
their meal!**

After Pocahontas was baptized in Virginia, her new name was

"The Lady Rebecca!"

In early Virginia, upper class boys had to learn good manners and leadership skills while lower class boys had to learn to farm or learn a trade such as carpentry. Both classes may have had to learn hunting skills.

In early Virginia, upper class girls were prepared for marriage while lower class girls became household servants or sometimes, seamstresses!

According to the writings of John Smith, there was a man who hated his wife and killed her, cutting her into pieces and hiding her in different parts of his house.

When the woman was missing, the man's house was searched and parts of her body were discovered.

The man's excuse was that he was starving and had to satisfy his hunger.

The man was burned for his horrible act!

At Historic Jamestowne, there is an Archaearium, a museum built to house and display artifacts from the ongoing archaeological digs at the site! Archaearium is a made-up word! It has a made-up definition, too: an archeological excavation which is covered by a glass building!

Other Items Found...

While digging in the Jamestown area, archaeologists have found what is known as an ear picker. It is made of silver and shaped like a dolphin. It has two ends. The pointed end was used to clean teeth and nails. The other spoon-shaped end was used to remove ear wax. As disgusting as it may seem, the colonists would save their ear wax and use it to coat sewing thread to make it easier to sew with!

Can you dig it?

Clothmakers, tax officials and merchants would put lead seals onto finished cloth. These seals show archaeologists the cloth used by the colonists.

SOME TOOLS, SUCH AS THIMBLES, NEEDLES, PINS AND IRONS HAVE BEEN DUG UP AND WERE POSSIBLY USED BY THE ORIGINAL SEVEN TAILORS AT JAMESTOWN!

Fourteen thimbles have been uncovered. Eleven of them are made of brass. They all appear to have been made in Nuremberg, Germany. Nuremberg thimbles are usually tall and narrow with a flat top and bear decorative stamping around the border.

Armor for the colonists generally weighed more than 20 pounds and was made up of a helmet, breast plate and back plate. There were tassets that protected the upper thighs. Sometimes neck protection, called a gorget, would be worn.

ARCHAEOLOGISTS HAVE FOUND COINS THAT HAVE DATES ON THEM BUT THE DATES ARE NOT NECESSARILY ACCURATE. COINS COULD HAVE BEEN USED FOR MANY YEARS IN A PLACE LIKE JAMESTOWN WHERE THERE WAS A SHORT SUPPLY.

In the 17th century, the time of the Jamestown colony, people ate using knives, spoons and hands. The fork was not commonly used by Englishmen until more than 100 years after the founding of Jamestown!

During the archaeological digs at Jamestown, many fish hooks of all sizes have been found. Settlers would use the fish hooks to catch many different kinds of fish from the James River.

Archaeologists have found the skeleton of a young European male between the ages of 19 and 22. The skeleton had a musket ball lodged in its lower right leg that fractured bones and ruptured a major artery below the knee. The young man would have bled to death in minutes!

Archaeologists have found quite a number of buried bodies. Many of the burials seem to be hurried and sloppy. The bodies were tossed into graves that were smaller than the bodies. Some of the bodies were clothed, which was unheard of at the time because clothing was recycled. It has been suggested that the settlers may not have wanted to touch the clothing for fear of getting sick and dying themselves!

A part of a wood instrument like a recorder was found dating back to 1610. Recorders were easy to play and were used by street musicians, and in church and theater music.

A brass cymbal from a tambourine was found. Music was very important to the settlers. Most people sang and would accompany themselves with a lute or a tambourine.

More than a dozen gaming dice have been found during the digs. Most are made of bone but two are made of ivory and one is lead.

Pass-dice was a popular game in which two players would try to throw doubles.

Every die that has been found has been the size of a pencil eraser! They are thought to be so little so that the settlers could hide the forbidden dice from their superiors!

A lead figurine was found of a boy who appears to be dancing. It is possible that it was a toy brought along for the amusement of an adult or a child at the colony. The object could have also been intended for trade with the Indians.

A pair of iron pliers has been found that were possibly used to make sheet copper into pendants and beads for trade with the Virginia Indians.

A doublet is a close-fitting men's jacket that is fastened together by rows of small round buttons. Over 150 doublet buttons have been found during the digs!

MANY BRASS BUCKLES HAVE BEEN FOUND AT THE SITE OF THE FORT THAT WERE USED TO FASTEN BELTS AT THE WAIST, SWORD BELTS, ARMOR BELTS, AND SPURS.

SCUPPET– AN ENTRENCHING TOOL USED TO
BUILD DEFENSIVE STRUCTURES

FELLING AXE – HAS A LONG NARROW BLADE USED
TO CHOP DOWN TREES AND CUT
OFF LIMBS

FUNNEL– MAY HAVE BEEN USED TO GRIND
GRAINS AND WAS LISTED AS A
NECESSARY PART OF A
SURGEON'S CHEST

COMPASS –CARPENTERS WOULD HAVE USED
THIS TO INSCRIBE CIRCLES AND ARCS
AND TO TRANSFER MEASUREMENTS

TRIANGULAR FILE –USED BY CARPENTERS TO
SHARPEN SAW TEETH

A copper alloy spur rowel with a silver coating was found, indicating that it was part of an expensive set of spurs. Spurs were a status symbol and gentlemen wore them at all times, even when they weren't riding horses!

During the digs, book clasps were found. Book clasps were attached to book covers to keep the books closed. To find these means that there were people at Jamestown who could read and write, and for the most part only gentlemen were educated at that time!

A tool called a spatula mundani was found during an archaeological dig. You might call it a "poop scoop!" The iron tool had a spatula on one end and a "spoon" with a round knob on the other end. It was used to cure constipation.

The "spoon" end was probably used to withdraw "poop" and the spatula was probably used to stir and apply preparations to the affected area!

One reason the colonists suffered from constipation was a lack of fruit and fresh vegetables!

Be sure you eat lots of fiber!

Can You Speak an Indian Language?

mockasins – shoes

pokatawer – fire

attonce – arrows

suckhanna – water

wingapoh or netoppew – friends

marrapough – enemies

necut – one

ningh – two

nuss – three

necuttweunquaogh – one thousand

ka ka torawincs yowo – What call you this?

tomahacks – axes

pamesacks – knives

mattassin – copper

pawcussacks – guns

Elizabethan English Words

Hoigh – high

Mought – might

Recken – believe

Salet – salad

Toide – tide

Smidgen – a bit

Tee-toncey – tiny

Chainy – china (dinnerware, not the country!)

Nary – not any

Elizabethan Tongue Twisters

The skunk sat on a stump and thunk the stump stunk but the stump thunk the skunk stunk.

Bluebirds bring bright berries.

She sheared six shabby sick sheep.

Say them fast three times!

About the Author

Carole Marsh is an author and publisher who has written many works of fiction and nonfiction for young readers. She is the founder and CEO of Gallopade International, established in 1979. Today, Gallopade International is widely recognized as the leading source of educational material for every state and many countries. Carole is the creator of the Virginia Experience Curriculum series that has raised test scores up to 400%! Carole loves books, libraries, museums, and "digging for trivia!" You can visit her websites at gallopade.com

Other Books in the Jamestown Series

The Mystery at Jamestown
Jamestown, America's First Permanent English Settlement
The Jamestown Storybook
Jamestown Readers: Captain John Smith, Pocahontas,
                    Queen Anne, Chief Powhatan, John Rolfe,
                    Christopher Newport, Thomas West, Lord De La Warr
Plus! A Jamestown Mural

Bibliography

BOOKS

Love and Hate in Jamestown by David A. Price
A Historical Album of Virginia by William Cocke
America the Beautiful—Virginia by Sylvia McNair
Virginia Women: The First Two Hundred Years by Anne Firor Scott and Suzanne Lebsock
Virginia—Compass American Guides by K. M. Kostyal
Colonial—The Story Behind the Scenery by James N. Haskett

WEB SITES

www.williamsburgprivatetours.com
http://www.pbs.org/wnet/secrets/case_jamestown/interview.html
http://www.apva.org
www.historyisfun.org
www.historicjamestowne.org
www.nps.gov
http://noahwebsterhouse.org/games/html
http://www.teachertools.org/documents/Chap4Trivia.htm
http://www.jamestown2007.org